T0114753

The Hyena Wears Darkness

Published by:

Luviri Press

P/Bag 201, Mzuzu

ISBN 978-99960-20-5

eISBN 978-99960-21-2

Front cover illustration © Alice Baer

Back cover photograph © Moira Chimombo

First published by WASI Publications in 2006

Printed in Malawi by Baptist Publications, P.O. Box 444, Lilongwe.

DEDICATION

To the survivors:
death is not the only end-point for the human experience

The Hyena Wears Darkness

Steve Chimombo

The impact of the HIV&AIDS pandemic on African societies steeped in risky cultural customs

Luviri Press
2017

By the Same Author

Poetry

Napolo Poems (Manchichi)
Napolo and the Python (Heinemann)
Epic of the Forest Creatures (WASI)
Breaking the Beadstrings (WASI)
Python! Python! (WASI)
The Vipya Poem (WASI)
Ndakatulo za Napolo (Manchichi)

Plays

The Rainmaker (Popular Publications)
Wachiona Ndani? (Dzuka)
Sister! Sister! (WASI)
Achiweni Wani? [translation of *Wachiona Ndani?* by A. Mbwana] (Manchichi)

Novels

The Basket Girl (Popular Publications)
The Wrath of Napolo (WASI)

Children's Literature

Caves of Nazimbuli (Popular Publications)
Child of Clay (Popular Publications)
Operation Kalulu (Popular Publications)
The Bird Boy's Song (WASI)
Fire on Kaphirintiwa (WASI)

Short Stories

Tell me a Story (Dzuka)

Folklore

Malawian Oral Literature (Center for Social Research)
Napolo ku Zomba (Manchichi)

Criticism

The Culture of Democracy [with Moira Chimombo] (WASI)

General

Directory of Malawian Writing (Dept of Arts and Crafts)

ACKNOWLEDGEMENTS

"The Widow's Liberation" was accepted for publication in *Inspiration Magazine*. However, the edition it was to appear in had not come out as we went to press. "The Widow's Revenge" appeared first in *Mawu Magazine*, Number 2, Issue 1, 2006, pp 22-23, 27. "The Hyena Wears Darkness" appeared first in *WASI: the magazine for the arts*, Volume 16, Number 2, April 2006, pp 18-25.

Although published separately, the stories form a unit I am calling ambitiously a trilogy. The first story generated the rest at different times, but during the same period of inspiration. However, each story was meant, and was published, to stand on its own. Hence, after the initial story, the sequels had to have initial background information not available for readers who had not read the previous stories.

I decided to reproduce the stories as they were originally written. The background material for the sequels, it will be discovered, has been integrated in a manner to reduce redundancies. In fact, it still serves similar purposes, especially for such long stories, now serving as "chapters" in a novelette.

Steve Chimombo, 2006

Second Edition

I am most grateful to Prof Klaus Fiedler for suggesting this second edition of *The Hyena Wears Darkness*. I know that my late husband would have been pleased to have it appear at this time, given the resurfacing of interest in cultural practices that have contributed to the spread of HIV, as well as the message of hope that the treatment has provided.

Moira Chimombo, April 2017

CONTENTS

INTRODUCTION TO THE FIRST EDITION

Some people often ignore the fact that writers respond to the HIV&AIDS pandemic by using it as a theme in their poetry, fiction, and plays. Apart from succumbing to the pandemic itself—writers are also human beings—the pen is their best tool for responding. I started recording the writers' responses as early as 1990, when I wrote 'AIDS and the Writer' in *WASI: the magazine for the arts*. The article reported the results of a poetry competition organized by the Ministry of Health on the theme. There have been other competitions also by different institutions since then. Some radio and television programs have also called upon the writer to help in the dissemination of information to their listeners.

The response has been quantifiably impressive. Witness the ever-recurring theme in the newspapers and magazines. Some of the fiction has found its way into collections published by the Malawi Writers Union. Recently funding has also been made available to keep the writers contributing. For example, National Library Service, with funding from the National AIDS Commission, is now buying and distributing publications on the theme. The Malawi Writers Union is also putting together creative writing on HIV&AIDS for more anthologies to be published.

The Hyena Wears Darkness is my own contribution to this massive national campaign to educate the public on the pandemic. Its focus is on those cultural practices which help propagate HIV&AIDS in our own society. Practices like *kuchotsa fumbi*, the ritual deflowering of initiates, or the practical tests done by their male counterparts; *kusudzula*, the sexual cleansing of the widow or widower; or *kulowa kufa*, widow inheritance. There are many more such practices, but these are the main, most prevalent ones up and down the country, regardless of ethnic background, as research on the subject has revealed.

In this novelette, I explore a family's plight in the face of an infected male. Before he dies he passes the infection on to his wife. The society requires that, at the death of a spouse, the survivor has to undergo a cleansing ceremony. The ceremony involves a relative or hired person to have sex with the survivor. In this case, the widow may have passed the virus on to another person outside the immediate family. It is a vicious chain reaction that involves the unborn, too, and ultimately the whole society and the nation.

In "The Widow's Liberation," the main character is nominated to perform the sexual cleansing with his brother's widow. "The Widow's Revenge" carries the situation a step further by having the widow reacting to the violation of her body. The fact that HIV&AIDS is depopulating the society forces both the government and the upholders of traditional customs, in "The Hyena Wears Darkness," to re-examine those practices deemed to propagate the virus. As such the novelette is really a case study or a microcosm of what is happening in the real, larger world when a multisectoral approach is adopted to combat the pandemic.

The stories are also about life beyond the death of a spouse: how the survivors—the partner, the relatives and their societies—cope with the event. The widow is central to this event. She has to cope with her own individual loss and the cultural demands, which in this case are destructive to her well-being. The stories are dramatizations of the widow's realities.

Underlying the stories are elements of hope: hope, for the survival of the remnants, that in the face of these life-threatening practices HIV&AIDS will not triumph. Death should not be the only avenue for human experience.

The widow's liberation

1

Sigele Jika parked the pick-up by the turnoff to the little church at the top of Mutopa Hill. Sigele's pick-up was carrying Pangapatha's coffin with some of the closest female relatives at the back. Atupele, the widow, and her mother, with another woman, sat with him in front. It was while the women were getting out that Sigele wondered again about the sores on Atupele's wrists and feet. Surely, he reflected as he, too, climbed out, they can't be scabies.

Sigele's reflections were drowned by the women's wailings, which commingled distressingly with the hymns sung by two groups separated by the procession of mourners. The front group was of the uniformed *Mvano* women leading the reverend and the church elders. The one trailing at the back was the local church choir: a band of teenagers of both sexes. Unfortunately, the two groups sang different songs simultaneously as if they belonged to separate denominations. In any case, the young choristers sang their latest composition, which had yet to enter the hymnals. Not wanting to be outdone by the group ahead, they sang lustily:

> *How come?*
> *All your friends are dead*
> *But you're still around*
> *How come?*

The dirt track to the top of Mutopa was rough and steep. Sigele started breathing in short spurts after the first thirty meters. Mutopa Hill itself was on the slopes of the bigger and higher Mtalika Mountain. The congregation had attempted to clear the track of grass, stumps, and boulders. Only the grass and rocks were amenable to their treatment. The boulders and gullies remained. The tropical October sun beat on the coffin bearers' heads as they negotiated the coffin round these obstacles. Sigele, sweating freely and almost wheezing halfway up the hill, wondered how the pall bearers managed to do it. He did not dare to volunteer with the carrying. His leg and thigh muscles threatened to bring about cramps. They didn't feel strong enough to support his flabby stomach. Why did people build their churches on hills or mountains? Didn't they think of occasions such as these?

In school or college, Sigele had steered clear of the sports and athletic clubs. He gravitated toward the students' union tuck shops and bars. There he could perform his duties sitting, standing, or leaning against the counter. You only needed biceps and triceps to raise or lower a drink. His school friends had been in the Zero Zero Squad. At college, he had belonged to the Terrible Trio, that band whose slogan was drinks, dances, and dames. Such activities told on him now, at fifty.

The church choir behind him didn't seem to feel the incline or the heat. They resumed their marching song.

Sigele punctuated their song with snorts and pants. His shirt clung dripping all over his torso, his lungs were burning. By the time they came to the clearing that surrounded the church, he was ready to collapse.

He let the coffin bearers and procession enter the church. He looked for a place outside to sit without fainting. There was no refuge on the narrow *khonde*. Others had beaten him to it. There were boulders and more scattered around the church, but they were in the direct path of the searing sun. All the same, he had to sit down to relieve his leg and thigh muscles. He sweated and panted and wriggled on a boulder, envying those who sat under the trees a distance away. He couldn't join them, of course. He was supposed to be inside, with the relatives, close to the coffin. And for the hundredth time Sigele asked himself why he had permitted himself to be involved in the Ndamo family's living and dead.

2

It had been close to midnight when Sigele was woken up by the phone.

"I'm Mrs Atupele Ndamo," a woman's voice came over the wires. Your brother Pangapatha has been admitted at the Thanzi Clinic. I'm with him."

"How come you are in Mtalika?" Sigele asked, as if that was an immediate issue. Pangapatha worked in Kamba City, seventy kilometers away.

"We were coming from Ngwangwa, where we went to seek traditional medicine. On our way back, your brother got worse and worse. We had to get off the bus to see Dr Mitsitsi. He is an old friend of your brother."

Sigele didn't need to ask why she had contacted him in the first place. The "your brother" was quite heavy.

"How bad is he?"

"The doctor says he can travel tomorrow but to go to one of the big Kamba hospitals for tests."

"What time do you intend to go?"

"Anytime in the morning but Pangapatha has been asking for you all this time. That's why I phoned."

"It's kind of late now, if he's in no immediate danger," Sigele came to a sudden decision. "I'll come round before 8 in the morning."

"Thank you so much." Atupele rang off.

Sigele tried to recover his shattered sleep. He had to reconcile several pieces of information arising from the phone call. The first one was that Pangapatha was the son of Ndamo, an older aunt's first born on Sigele's mother's side. Therefore, Pangapatha was more of a cousin than a brother according to their customs. The second one was that Uncle Ndamo himself had exiled himself in Njati, where he had married. He only emerged to visit his relatives back home at important funerals. The children in both villages hardly knew each other. Sigele had made overtures to know more of the Ndamo children when Pangapatha had come to Mtalika on a contract – he was in the construction business. Sigele had invited the other to dinner, which turned out to be a flop. They had no common background to start from. Even Sigele's journalistic training using interview techniques had elicited only monosyllables and one sentence responses. The invitation wasn't reciprocated by Pangapatha, either. This was the first time since that painful evening for Pangapatha to renew contact.

The resident owl in the *kachere* tree in Sigele's garden was still hooting heartily when he finally reconnected with the interrupted sleep.

The following morning found Sigele parking in front of Thanzi Clinic. He was directed to Ward C, where he found a nurse syringing Pangapatha's ears. A woman he took to be Atupele was holding the bowl under the patient's jaw. Pangapatha was propped against the headboard. The hot water flowed freely from his ear onto the bowl. That was when Sigele noticed the sores on the wrists holding the bowl against the patient's jaw line.

After the greetings from both women, Atupele introduced herself. They continued ministering to the patient. Sigele sat down on the adjacent bed and enquired after Pangapatha. The patient was too weak to respond for himself.

He found Atupele to be a plump, light-skinned woman in her late thirties. She had an ample bosom and an equally generous bottom. He discovered this as she fussed around her husband and helped the nurse in her duties.

Atupele wore a blue spotted blouse open at the neck. The sores had not touched that area. Below the multi-patterned *chitenje*, her ankles and feet were encased in black leather shoes. There were more of the sores down there too. Some were dry, others looked as if freshly opened. He wondered what they were.

"Is the doctor around?" Sigele was directed to the main wing of the clinic. He had been there before a number of times, with members of his family and the domestic staff. Even at midnight, during emergencies. Dr Mitsitsi had the drugs not available in the government hospital. The doctor told him the same thing Atupele had: thorough tests at a big hospital: blood, urine, stool the whole works.

"We need your help," Atupele told him when he resumed his seat on the bed in Ward C. The nurse was gone. He raised his head enquiringly.

"We have money only for transport back to Kamba," she continued. "There is no more where we are going. What we had has been spent on travel and traditional medicines around the country."

Sigele had given her K500. She received it rather reluctantly.

"We have five children," she began. "I don't know …"

Sigele had given her another K500. She put the two notes together and looked at them helplessly. It was the second time he had looked at her hands as they held the notes together. The marred skin of the wrists was visible.

Sigele did not add any more money to the "pin"—as a thousand kwacha was called colloquially. He had not come prepared for this. Even if he had more money he did not know why he had to be the family provider to a distant brother he hardly knew. It was the first time he had met Atupele, too, and he wondered how she could have the courage to ask for financial help from a virtual stranger.

"My husband told me about your dinner invitation." It was as if she had read his thoughts. "I couldn't come. I was in Kamba. He spoke highly of you."

Even then, Sigele thought, that was not enough reason to extract money from me. He looked at her again. The full lips trembled slightly. She averted her eyes.

"Thank you for helping us so much." She spoke softly. "This money will see us through for the next few days."

Sigele was unmoved. He did not see himself recultivating the acquaintance, either. He had done the only decent thing in the circumstances. That should have been the close of the chapter. Apparently, it wasn't.

A week later Atupele had phoned: Pangapatha was admitted in hospital. Sigele had not taken any action. Two days ago, Atupele had phoned again: Pangapatha was dead.

"Could you please help us make the funeral arrangements?" Atupele pleaded.

"The people in the township you live in have got committees that do these things, don't they?" Sigele could see himself being thrown into another financial arrangement.

"Your brother joined the church but with his condition he couldn't keep it up. Still they are sending someone to keep the vigil. That's all."

"What about his father?" Sigele was furious.

"You know Uncle Ndamo is too old. He is too poor. The Njati people accepted him just because he was married there. Several times they tried to repatriate him, if that's the word for it, but he stuck there. You are the nearest blood brother."

"So now it's a question of where Pangapatha is to be buried and more precisely who is to foot the bill?"

"You know these things." There was a catch in her voice. "I can't ask my relatives because ours was a shotgun wedding. My father is dead. My uncle doesn't speak to me. My mother was only resigned to the fact a few years ago. She is coming to the funeral, though."

Sigele found himself driving his pick-up to meet Atupele at the mortuary.

3

The hymns stopped inside the church. The mourners, heads bowed, trooped out. The wailing resumed as the coffin was also carried out. The people sitting outside the church stood up. A detachment went to relieve the pall bearers after they had moved only twenty meters. Sigele sidled into the procession on its way to the graveyard. The pick-up would stay where it was till after the burial.

He discovered he was back in front of the young choristers. They too resumed their marching song:

> *How come?*
> *All your friends are gone*
> *But you're still around*
> *How come?*
> *Explain yourself, my brother.*

Sigele wondered why such a song had to be a favorite. Maybe the choir had a limited repertoire. However, it seemed as if they were asking him directly. Nevertheless, it set him thinking, too. To occupy his mind on the way to the graveyard he took an inventory of his college and school friends.

The Terrible Trio had gravitated towards each other as early as the orientation week the college had organized for the first years. The Trio was composed of Madipo, the Zimbabwean, Mudzipansi, from his own secondary school, and, of course, Sigele. Two or three others were loosely attached to them, but were not the hard core whose motto was drinks, dances, and dames. Academically they were brilliant, but their extracurricular activities were elsewhere.

The hangovers of the Terrible Trio's social activities persisted after graduation for some of them. Madipo died suddenly in Harare. Sigele never got the details of what had killed him. Mudzipansi came back wasted from South Africa, where he had worked for several years. He went straight into a private hospital where he vomited and evacuated incessantly till his death a few weeks later. Sigele was the last of the gang.

Sigele had lost track of his friends from secondary school. Some had dropped by the wayside. He was reminded of their existence, actually their exits, from the media's death notices, in memoriams or tombstone unveilings. There were numerous of them on the classified pages, splashed as lavishly as for other merchandize. In this manner, he filled himself in on where his ex-friends had been working, where they were buried, whether or not they had families, and even their original home villages and districts.

Sigele's mind couldn't easily go as far back as his primary school. Only one or two friends emerged. Sigele had invited Mwachitanji to his town home for a weekend. Mwachitanji had reciprocated and invited him to his village. Sigele vaguely remembered the evening meal followed by a folk story session with Mwachitanji's mother. The mother told them why the owl hooted in the manner he did.

Mr Owl, the story went, had two wives. The first wife fell ill and Owl was going to visit her when he heard that the second wife was also taken sick. Owl turned to go back to see the second wife when he got the message that his first wife was dead. He was rushing to the funeral when another message reached him that his second wife was dead too. Owl was left standing by the roadside crying "Hih! Hih!" Up to this day he doesn't know which funeral to attend first.

Mwachitanji's mother told them this was why the owl was associated with news of illnesses or death. Sigele didn't know whether or not his old friend was alive. The death notices were silent on him.

In this manner, Sigele endured the choir's song and the burial ceremony afterwards.

4

Sigele was relieved there was no singing after the burial. Singles and small groups detached themselves at the exit point to talk solemnly as they walked back to Mutopa village. Some branched off onto the several paths leading to the other villages.

This was also the time to catch up with familiar faces or relatives he had noticed around the graveyard but could not talk to under the circumstances. It was not surprising, therefore, for Uncle Ndamo to sidle up to him for, he hoped, casual conversation not possible when they were at the bereaved's house yesterday or this morning.

"You will be returning to Mtalika today?" It was more of a statement than a question.

"I have to get back to work." He turned to look at the slightly bent form. He must have been taller and stockier when young.

"We were afraid of that." There was a certain unwarranted grimness in the voice. "The *kusudzula* ceremony is scheduled for this evening. You will have to delay your departure until after that."

"As far as I know the *kusudzula* ceremony is held after the *lumeto*, the shaving of the hair. Why is it being held on the day of burial?"

"Things change, my son." A more pronounced grimness if not determination. "African customs have adapted to the western pace of life. Look at you. Here you are running away from the village soon after the burial. Atupele's mother, is here. You know they come from Mbamba. She has to go back by tomorrow, she said." Ndamo made another sound down his throat.

"Well, there isn't much to do here for those from other places, is there?" Sigele flared slightly. He wasn't going to be cajoled into staying longer than was necessary.

"In the olden times, anyone who left before a reasonable number of days had elapsed would be declared a witch. Or having killed the deceased. Now we are adapting to you town people."

"But the *kusudzula* ceremony is only between the closest members of the deceased's family. Why should I stick around for that? It's a long way back to Mtalika."

"You don't understand," Ndamo made the same guttural sound again. "Maybe it's your western upbringing. Maybe it's because we haven't lived together as a clan. You see me as a stranger. Yet kinship is like a bone, it does not rot."

Sigele could not fathom the direction the talk was taking. He wished the man would come to the point. Perhaps it was his uncle's village upbringing that made him talk round subjects.

"Well, the last time we met was at another funeral. We hardly talked to each other. I had to leave soon after the burial again."

"Exactly. It's like today." Ndamo cleared his throat. "Let me explain something to you. When I see you I see my son. You are like your departed brother there."

Ndamo pointed back to the graveyard. Only the *masuku* and *chitimbe* trees were visible. The procession, now too loose to be called that, was back on the dirt track that led to the little church on the hill and the village main road where Sigele had left his pick-up.

"There is no need to remind me of the relationship, uncle. I'm not as removed from you and our people's customs as you want to believe."

"Then you will understand what your people want you to do."

"What do they want me to do?" he checked himself before adding the "now".

"For you to *kusudzula* Atupele."

"What?" Sigele's mouth worked. It had gone dry suddenly. He missed a step but disguised it as sidestepping an outcrop on the road.

"You are the right person to do this." Ndamo shrugged his shoulders.

"But I'm not part of this village. Surely there are relatives in this village who can perform this?"

"Living apart from each other is actually a great help. Then you won't be shy with each other."

"Again, as far as I gather these things take a long time to prepare. There are the medicines to be found from the bush. The relatives of both sides have to agree."

"Those things have already been taken care of. The important relatives are here. Mrs Andaunire has brought the necessary medicines."

"She has what?"

"Andaunire is a businesswoman and interested in quick results. She told us she didn't have the time to come again on future dates for the *lumeto* and then for the *kusudzula* which usually take place on a separate occasion. Therefore, she came fully prepared to finalize the important rites, if we permitted her."

"And you did?"

"It is in the interest of both sides of the family to effect the rites as precipitately as possible."

This was uncharacteristic of village practice, Sigele thought.

"Following the western practice?" He couldn't help putting it in.

"We are forced by circumstances to adapt," Ndamo almost chuckled.

"But *kusudzula* includes having sex with the widow, doesn't it?" Sigele wanted to clarify the issues involved. He had a vision of his wife.

"It's just a duty on both sides to release the widow so she can marry again. You must admit in this case it is more than just a duty. Atupele is quite a woman, the epitome of womanhood. Several young men would jump at a chance like this."

"Why don't you let them, then?"

"You are the brother to the deceased. You have already helped the family a great deal. The widow seems to prefer this arrangement, too."

"Does she?" Sigele ejaculated. He was reminded of Atupele's sores again.

"She was appraised of the matter."

"Why wasn't I appraised of the matter, too?"

"We are doing it, now"

Sigele's mind whirled. He tried to remember the times he had sex outside his family. He had received several challenges but had remained clean. Before his marriage was a different matter altogether. He had to do research on who to marry from several willing candidates, he rationalized. At college again, casual sex was part of the extracurricular activities, as The Terrible Trio's slogan pronounced: drinks, dances, and dames.

"They sent me to prepare you for the event this evening," Ndamo went on relentlessly.

Sigele knew he wasn't prepared. Mechanically, he didn't have the condoms: who brought them to funerals, anyway? Funerals were "cool" periods when no sex was permitted. Everyone observed this fact for fear of the *mwikho* taboo. Yet here were the same people forcing, yes, forcing him to violate the taboo. Not only that, to have skin to skin sex, as his friends called it, with his brother's widow.

Sigele knew he wasn't prepared. Emotionally, he didn't feel the urge for sex as strongly as he used to in school or college. After marriage, he had settled down to regular performances which he found satisfying enough without seeking external aid. Moreover, if he consented to see the ceremony through, the fact that the whole village knew and expected him to do it detracted from any desire on his part.

Atupele was indeed delectable, but somehow Sigele couldn't see himself rising up to the occasion in such a public act.

"Well, here is your car," Ndamo said with forced heartiness. "We'll meet again after the washing of the hoes."

"Aren't you coming with us?"

"The car is already full with your women."

It was indeed. The same mourners and more beside had positioned themselves on top. Atupele, Mrs Andaunire and the other women waited outside the passenger side.

Sigele fumbled ostentatiously with the car keys. He got the passenger door open and fled to his side. When he looked through his window he noticed that Atupele was to sit next to him again. Sigele shivered.

"Hello, brother." It was Ndakulapa, his elder brother.

"Oh, so you're here, too. I thought I saw your face in the crowd at the graveyard." Ndakulapa had retired, too, to his wife's village. He only emerged at funerals and weddings.

"They phoned me. I thought you shouldn't shoulder the family burdens alone, young as you are. You have already done a lot for them."

It was a joke between them to kid Sigele when they met, even at his age.

"I must say," was all Sigele could find to say. He didn't see himself recounting the latest demand.

"I will join Uncle Ndamo, then. There's no room for me in your pick-up. We'll meet again."

"When are you going back?"

"You know me." Ndakulapa laughed. "Maybe tomorrow or even the day after. I do get involved in these village things."

Sigele had to turn the car round and retrace the route to the village. He checked that the gear was in neutral. The movement brought the back of his wrist against Atupele's thigh. He recoiled. She brought her arm down as if to push her knees together. She too brushed against him. The sores were prominent on her wrist. He breathed deeply. He turned on the engine and released the brakes. His wrist and elbow brushed against her waist and thigh again. He shrank back. He pushed the accelerator pedal down softly as he released the clutch for the first time.

Several mourners on foot stopped or stepped aside to let the pick-up turn round in the narrow road. Each change of gear brought Sigele's wrist or elbow against Atupele. Each contact brought out an involuntary recoil from him. There was sweat on his brows, palms, and armpits as if he was climbing up the hill to the little church again.

No, Sigele determined, the sores were too small for scabies. They were too widespread for casual or accidental scratches or cuts for that matter. In any case, they wouldn't be on both wrists and ankles. They looked like Kaposi's sarcoma. Yes, Sigele jerked up, that was what he was trying to remember from the pictures and other victims of them. They could only be that. This suggested also what Pangapatha had died of. Dr Mitsitsi had not wanted to say it outright. The speaker at the funeral who had given Pangapatha's profile had also been vague about the causes of death. He only talked about how the deceased had suffered and tried all the known cures from western and African medicines. Pangapatha had given up after a long struggle. Sigele shuddered violently. He must have groaned aloud.

"Are you all right, in-law?" Atupele turned glistening red eyes on him. They gazed profoundly at each other. He almost melted.

"I just can't get over the fact that Pangapatha is gone," he said hastily. "It is only last week that I saw him at Thanzi Clinic with you."

He stifled a sob that threatened to erupt with a dry cough. The heart overworked the ventricles inside him.

"You will have us crying all over again." Atupele leaned towards him, the hot full lips quivering. "We're tired of crying. Let's look to the future."

He looked at the black band she had tied round her head. Her hair was hidden under a headcloth. She looked the model of caged womanhood. It was tempting to cradle her head in comforting arms and stroke those lovely cheeks. Sigele gnashed his teeth and gripped the wheel more tightly.

He concentrated on his driving. However, he was acutely aware of the plump body brushing and bumping against him from shoulder to calf on the uneven surface of the road. Sigele wondered which was worse, this present physical torment or the promised erotic ordeal a few hours later. Why did Chauta let him live long enough to face this trial? He had never been placed in such a situation as this before. He remembered his college days again. Yes, but those were the reckless youthful days. They were the daring adventure stories to share the morning after with his friends.

Sigele had managed to live a relatively quiet married life. He might not have entered a connubial paradise but it had yielded half a dozen Jikas. Two of them had made him a grandfather. Two were still in college. The other two were about to finish high school. Not a bad five-decade venture, at all. Now here was this ultimate trial in his life, from an unexpected and somewhat irresistible quarter. At fifty, he whimpered to himself, he shouldn't cry.

A chameleon detached itself from a shrub on one side of the road. It took a tentative step on the hot dusty road. A round socket with a tiny hole for an eye rolled and looked at the pick-up. Defiantly it started to cross the road. It lifted a front and back leg, wavered and planted them forward. The other set followed faster as the pick-up neared. It was almost running as the vehicle passed it. It disappeared in the grass. Sigele remembered the children's song

> *Chameleon, why are your eyes swollen?*
> *There are funerals at home.*
> *Look at my homestead:*
> *It's empty, empty, empty.*

> *I shall leave this village,*
> *You stay behind and rebuild it.*
> *Do not laugh children:*
> *It's empty, empty, empty.*

No, at fifty he shouldn't cry, like the chameleon. There was so much to live for. He looked forward to another decade of fruitful life.

He had survived so much in his young days. He had to keep on surviving to his natural life span, not on ARVs, he determined. But now how could he escape Atupele by his side?

5

The owners of the funeral, that is, the closest relatives to the deceased, congregated in Uncle Ndamo's sitting room. The men sat on the available furniture. The women sat on a mat on the floor. The gloom of the room was relieved by a small paraffin lamp placed centrally on the table. It was enough to illuminate the ten or so sombre faces around. The last two items on the unannounced agenda were very well understood: the disposal of the deceased's property and the release of the widow for future matrimony.

Sigele sat as a non-contributor for the first item. Pangapatha's people argued vociferously: they wanted a share of their son's accumulated property. They had housed, educated, and protected the deceased till adulthood. He had accumulated some of his property long before he got married. The widow's arguments were condensed in a piece of paper Atupele found among her husband's effects: the house and its contents were to go to his wife and children. The arguments went round and round until Mrs Andaunire declared a middle view: some of the property would be shared with the Ndamos at Atupele's discretion. The Ndamos conceded grudgingly. Everyone was relieved: they did not have to go to court, after all.

"Is the medicine ready?" Uncle Ndamo's question introduced the last item for the evening.

"It is ready," Mrs Andaunire answered.

Atupele excused herself politely and went out.

"Let us proceed, then," Uncle Ndamo cleared his throat. "Some people have to leave for far off places soon after."

Everyone looked at Sigele, including Ndakulapa, his brother. Sigele roused himself. His earlier panic had left him shaken but he was determined to make his point before leaving.

"I believe we are all following our ancestors' customs here," he began. "The *kusudzula* ceremony, I understand has been brought forward because of the complications of having to meet again at some other date. However, if we are still following tradition and performing the *kusudzula* rite as it should be done then I would like to alter today's arrangement for conformity."

The gathering was attentive. They had not expected a speech, only speedy compliance.

"The earlier arrangement that I should participate was made before Ndakulapa, my elder brother, arrived for the funeral. Now that he is here, I'm relinquishing the role. Ndakulapa is the Jika family's representative, the *nkhoswe* or the ambassador, as the eldest brother. I'm leaving everything in his hands. That is all I had to say."

Sigele looked at Ndakulapa. He thought he saw a twist of mockery in his brother's expression. It was as if he was saying: Typical. He turned to Uncle Ndamo. Did he detect pity in the old man's face? He got up without waiting for an answer. No one said anything as he passed the elders and went outside.

He didn't know where Atupele was. Perhaps waiting for him now in one of the houses.

The fire outside the bereaved house was still smouldering. There would be another ceremony to quench it, too, at some point, he thought, as he walked past it to his pick-up by the roadside. As he drove away, Sigele couldn't get rid of the young choristers' marching song still haunting the sound track of his mind:

> *How come?*
> *Your relatives are dying*
> *But you are still alive.*
> *How come?*

The widow's revenge

1

"Is the medicine ready?" Uncle Ndamo asked as if to no one in particular.

"It is ready" Mrs Andaunire, Atupele's mother answered.

It was Atupele's cue to leave the room. With a raging heart, she lifted herself heavily from the mat. The sob she stifled was not because of Pangapatha, her late husband, whom they had all helped to bury that afternoon. It was the helpless anger that these elderly people—Uncle Ndamo heading her husband's relatives and Mrs Andaunire the only person representing the widow's side—had all consented to the *kusudzula* ceremony she had to go through now.

"Be prepared for the *kusudzula* this evening," her mother had warned her.

"I thought the ceremony takes place months or even a year later."

"You know I'm managing Andaunire Enterprises alone now. I can't afford a day away from the business. I'm losing too much as I stand here."

"How can I bury my husband in the afternoon and then go through the *kusudzula* the same evening?"

"Listen, I only came to this funeral because you are my daughter. Your father, even if he was alive, wouldn't have come. Your uncle refused to come with me even when I offered him the transport. You know the reasons why. In any case, I don't want to have to come here again, ever, even for the *kusudzula*, if you don't want to go through it today."

"Does the Ndamo side know about this?" Atupele couldn't see herself coming to Mutopa village alone at some future date even for the *sadaka*, either.

"I've told them what I told you." Her mother was firm. "I brought the medicine in anticipation of this. So be ready for the man."

Of course, the elders also knew, in fact, had already chosen which of her in-laws she was to consummate the rite with. Sigele Jika, her mother told her, as if she was telling her which man would take her shopping. Sigele Jika, the same man who had selflessly helped the couple financially in Pangapatha's last dying days. It was Sigele, sitting almost dejectedly a little away from the male elders around the table, who had also bought the coffin and transported the body to Mutopa village in his pick-up. He had continued to be transport officer till the burial this afternoon. Now they had requested him to perform this last ceremony, too. How much can relatives ask of a man?

As she got up, Atupele did not look at the other half a dozen or so elders around the table. Her foot caught in the folds of her *chitenje*. She stumbled and held onto her mother's shoulder, sitting on the same mat as the other elderly women. Her mother did not offer to lead her outside as the other women had done at the last evening of the deceased. Atupele had been hysterical then. "My husband! Who is going to take care of the children?" she had wailed. They had trudged from the bereaved's house to join the coffin on Sigele's pick-up since the service was to be held in the little church on Mutopa Hill. In her unsteady walk to the pick-up, she had also been led by a group of supportive women.

It had been like this up to the laying of the wreaths, when she broke down and had to be half-carried away from the mound, now looking flamboyant with the multicolored flowers from relatives, friends, and colleagues.

No, no supportive woman led her outside. The last widow's rite was all her own with the appointed man. There the women sat unmoving and, it seemed, even unmoved by what was going to happen to her. Bowed greying heads, cupped palms under chins, legs folded to one side in the characteristic pose of the African village woman. In that pose the trunk was always leaning to one side, lopsidedly. The women refused resolutely even eye contact with her.

Atupele now knew why sacrificial animals going to slaughter bleated, she thought bleakly holding back another flood of tears as she emerged from Uncle Ndamo's house.

2

It was now quite dark outside. The fire in front of the bereaved's house was dying. Someone must stoke it before it died out entirely, Atupele looked around as if that was the most urgent thing to do. Where was everyone? There had been all night singing in and around the bereaved's house. Now it was silent. The affairs of the funeral were left with the owners of the village. She was one of the affairs of the village. Atupele continued her solitary walk to Agogo's hut. The heat and dryness of the air were still there in the air. At least it was free air outside, rather than the musty inside she had just left.

Atupele walked over uneven bare ground covered with patches of *kapinga* grass. She had walked over the same route several times since she came with the body. Attempts at making lawns and flower gardens in the village were not always successful. The results were sometimes stumbling blocks between crowded houses, kitchens, bathrooms, and even animal or chicken sheds.

She knew where Agogo's hut lay. It was where they had tried to make her eat the food they had prepared for the mourners. She couldn't eat any. In fact, she hadn't eaten anything since coming to Mutopa village. She didn't feel hungry, only drained of energy. And emotion. And even will power.

She climbed the *khonde* of Agogo's hut. It was only one step up and forward to the thin pine door. She turned the handle and entered the yawning door. It was darker here. It smelt of dry dust and ash. It held the permanent odor of a windowless hut whose only ventilation was the door. It had the same feel as her own grandmother's at Mbamba on the lakeshore.

She held out her hands in front of her to meet any objects in her progress inside. She stepped to her right, along the wall. After a few steps, she bumped against a bed post. She leaned down and felt the frame all along to the very end. There was what felt like a small table beside the bed. She felt on top and brushed against a matchbox. That's better, she could at least light up the place.

The flare revealed a small tin lamp on the table. Atupele lit it and surveyed the room again. Nothing much. There was the single bed, the table, and a folding chair. A storage basket and a pot stood on one side of an empty fireplace in the center of the room. A rolled-up reed mat stood near the door. There were some clothes hanging on a string strung under the rafters from one end to the other. It looked desolate.

Some of Atupele's happiest moments were spent in her own grandmother's hut at Mbamba. After the evening meal, the children would gather round her fireplace seated on the firestones, a mat, or even her bed, roasting maize or potatoes, telling stories or throwing riddles. Whenever she had done some mischief she'd end up in her grandmother's hut. It was a place of refuge. The only place at home, in fact, she felt free. Grandmother treated her like a human being. Unformed maybe but lovable. There Atupele would lie snuggled against her grandmother after the fire had died out. How far away it was now from that hut, but so different. Only she had come in for a necessary ritual. Necessary for whom?

"Do I have to go through all this?" Atupele had asked her mother. "I didn't go through all the initiation ceremonies as I grew up since we lived mostly in town. Only the first and the last one. Why do I have to do this?"

"Every widow has to go through this or else she's not free to marry again."

"But I don't want to marry another man. Pangapatha was everything to me. That's why I married him even against you and father's wishes. After him I shall remain single for the rest of my life."

"There are other reasons behind the ritual, my daughter. It's not only to set you free."

"What reasons, mother?"

"Don't start giving me headaches again as you did when you got pregnant in school and ran away to get married. All the elders here have been through it, man or woman. All of them. They expect you to go through it too or we're going to have a case on our hands."

"Did they *kusudzula* you too?"

"Don't you remember Uncle Mbungo coming home to collect his brother's property? That's not all he came for."

Atupele didn't know all the details. She only remembered Uncle Mbungo coming over one long afternoon. Uncle Mbungo rarely visited them even when father was alive. This time he behaved like he was a regular visitor. Her mother behaved strangely too, like a little girl again. They were like marriageable cousins. It went on like this at the meal and afterwards. Then Uncle sent Atupele to buy groceries down the road. This was a two-kilometer return trip. When Atupele returned, Uncle had departed. What about the groceries? she had asked. He bought those for us, her mother had explained. Atupele went into the house to find it half-empty. Where was all the furniture? We've shared it with your father's relatives, mother said. Together with the bicycle? Of course, what are we women going to do with it? Atupele's heart sank. She didn't want to remind her mother that they could have sold it themselves to add on to what now looked like a hard future for them financially. Atupele had kept quiet.

Of course, her mother had gone through the *kusudzula* ceremony. It had included the distribution of the deceased's property. Just like what Atupele was going through now as custom demanded.

3

Atupele was undecided for a few moments. Should they use Agogo's bed. It was a single bed and might not withstand much agitation. The mat? It would be hard on the bare floor. She settled for Agogo's bed. It sounded outrageous but she reckoned if the custom came from the elders it made sense to perform it where the likes of Agogo slept. She sat on the bed dejectedly.

Atupele had not told her mother the real reason she couldn't marry again. Pangapatha had made her promise not to or else he wasn't going to write the last letter that served as the will that evening when the distribution of wealth was contested. In fact, it had been no accident that the letter was discovered among her husband's effects. Her husband had not been doing too well in the construction business. The government tenders he used to enjoy in the first republic were no longer forthcoming. He discovered it was because he was in the wrong party.

Before long he was reduced to building petty traders' one-roomed groceries or bottle stores. His illness drained him the other way too, as he had to keep track of who the next best medicine man was. He sold his pick-up and resorted to public transport and sleeping in dingy rest houses. Atupele grew alarmed as she observed themselves getting more and more destitute. They had their own house, of course, but then there were the water and electricity bills. Four of the children were in school. One in secondary. Another joining the next year. The last one starting primary school next year, too. And the food and the clothes to be bought.

Meanwhile Pangapatha grew weaker and more helpless. Atupele persuaded her husband to write a letter addressed to her.

"Do you think I'm dying?" Pangapatha had protested.

"We are all going to die, eventually," Atupele had pointed out. "Even if we live long enough we must have a record of how we want our property to be distributed when we go."

"But I'll leave everything to you and the children."

"That's what you say, and I believe you. But your relatives won't believe me when I tell them the same thing. Look at what happened to Andilandazonse, our neighbor. The father, uncle, and brothers came in a truck to clear the house and chase her out. She was left with only the clothes on her back, a few pots and plates. Even the children went to live with their grandfather in the village. Do you want that to happen to us?"

"Do you love me?"

"You know I do."

"Will you marry another man when I'm gone?"

"I couldn't think of doing that. Why?"

"Well, then, I will write this letter only if you promise to remain single all the rest of your life. You know I love you, too."

"I promise I will do as you wish."

It was true Atupule loved her husband. She remembered the time Pangapatha came to her secondary school to do some extension work to the buildings. Somehow, he had timed his trips to Mbamba trading centre to coincide with her going home after school. It all started with: Do you want a lift? At first Atupele said no. Pangapatha persisted. She gave in after a while: it was a five or so kilometer walk home otherwise.

It was a straight lift in the early days. Then the journey became interrupted by stopovers at a superette in Mbamba. A drink and a packet of biscuits. It went on like this till the invitation to the lakeshore resort where Pangapatha was staying. As the saying goes, one thing led to another, till she found herself pregnant. The school couldn't keep her. Nor could her father. Her grandmother had died by this time. She joined Pangapatha at the resort till he fulfilled his contract. She then went with him to Kamba city. Her father disowned her. Her mother relented only for the *chisamba* ceremony: You are still my daughter, I carried you inside me. I, too, had to go through the *chisamba* ceremony, she had told Atupele.

Her mother arranged the *chisamba* with other expectant women in another village. Her father didn't know but then he died a few years later. Atupele and her mother kept loose contact with each other after her father's death.

Atupele kept her mother posted on the appearance of her grandchildren. There was Ayami after Awechete. Then Ndemile …. Her mother was rather indifferent to the additions. She only started showing concern when Atupele reported Pangapatha's deteriorating health and their doing the rounds of clinics and medicine men. Atupele was very grateful for her mother's concern, otherwise she would have had no one on her side.

4

Atupele wondered whether or not to keep the little lamp on. She blew it out decisively. This ritual should happen in darkness, she thought. It would be like the *kuchotsa fumbi*, the ritual deflowering of nubile girls after their first initiation ceremony. The *fisi* or hyena, the deflowerer, came in the night, unannounced. He performed his duties silently and departed anonymously. Only in her case she would know who it was. Even though she knew who it was she preferred not having to watch herself being violated, for that was what it amounted to.

There was a smell like singed hair when she blew the lamp out. Then she was plunged into thick darkness. The door was still open but she could not see the smouldering outside fire anymore. Perhaps it was because she had moved from light to darkness too rapidly. Her eyes had yet to adjust.

Atupele pulled the blouse over her head while seated, being careful not to bruise the sores around her wrists. She shrugged her shoulders free of the straps of the bra she was wearing. She turned it back to front. It was always difficult to unclasp it from the back. She unclasped it and let it fall on her lap. She untied the headband, too. Her straightened hair frothed out. Some of it caressed her neck, collarbones, and shoulder blades.

She untied the *chitenje* and spread it around her on the bed. There was only a *mkeka* mat on the bed. Agogo's blanket was on the string above her. In any case, it would not have been decent to do it on top of Agogo's blanket. Her own *chitenje* would absorb all the mess.

Atupele stood up and hooked her thumbs on top of her pants and pulled them down. They slithered down to her ankles. She sat down again. She removed her right shoe with the big toe of the other foot. She reversed the procedure for the remaining shoe. She freed the feet from the pants by lifting them and shaking them off, careful not to bruise the sores on her ankles. She let the pants lie where they were and put her feet down again. Her bare feet felt the hard, dry mud flooring. She pushed the bra on the floor to join the pants.

Atupele was naked. She felt her breasts. The nipples were hard but cold. She was cold inside herself too, shrunken within her womanhood.

She put her elbows on her thighs and hugged her knees together. She put her head to her knees feeling her cold breasts and tits on her cold thighs.

It was not the idea of having sex with a strange man that shattered her most. It was the fact that her mother, yes, and all those elders in that house, had planned it all for her. Yes, they had conspired that she should do it without asking for her consent that had killed something within her. Interestingly enough, *kusudzula* was one of the things the elders never told the growing girls to be on the lookout for at the initiation ceremonies. Not even at the wedding *mwambo* ceremony that should one of them die first this is what was in store for the survivor.

Of course, she had heard of *kusudzula* before, but it was only hearsay. It happened to other women, not her. When Pangapatha died, it still had not entered her mind till her mother told her to prepare for it. Then things started exploding inside her. She spent the rest of the time weeping for her husband and for herself. As she lay in the foetal position, an image of her father came to her.

She must have been six or so. She heard her father chanting in front of a bush near the garden.

> Chelule, *go to sleep!*
> Chelule, *go to sleep!*

Atupele thought it strange for such an elderly person to be chanting the silly song as she and her friends did in the playground. Her father was peering under the umbrella formed by the shrubbery. She wanted to see what he could see there.

"Don't come any nearer," her father warned furiously. "You'll frighten it away."

"What is it father?" she hissed back at him.

"The *chelule* bird."

Her father was chanting to a bird in the depths of the foliage. It kept fluttering up and around from one branch to another, then drooping as if it was tired and going to sleep. It hopped up again, then drooped, as if it would fall off the branch, weary with sleep.

"*Chelule*, go to sleep!" her father chanted earnestly, if not desperately. Her father at last suddenly threw a stone he had in his hand. The bird disentangled itself from the branches and flew away to the freedom of the skies.

"What were you doing, father?"

"The *chelule* bird can be caught by chanting to it to go to sleep. If you chant long enough you can even capture it with your bare hands. Today I was not so lucky."

Atupele felt like the little *chelule* bird. The funeral songs had made her soporific. Her mind was fuzzy. She was ready to pass out and to be easy prey to the traditional customs closing upon her. She'd better not be caught napping. But how was she going to get out of this one?

5

Atupele raised her trunk, slid her arms outwards and downwards on the bed to retrieve the loose ends of her *chitenje*. She stood up slowly and wrapped herself all the way to the armpits. It felt like a shroud. Pangapatha must have been wrapped up like she was, only more permanently. She chilled at the thought.

Perhaps, Atupele clung to a stray thought, to avoid the pain of penetration she ought to want to enjoy what was to come. After all, she reassured herself, she did not find Sigele Jika unattractive in spite of his age. Furthermore, her husband hadn't been able to fulfil his marital obligations toward the end, as he got sicker and weaker. Perhaps the feel of a man inside her would do something positive to her, after what she had been through. It would be something of a reward to Sigele, too, after what *he* had been through to help them. She recalled her first encounter with Sigele.

It was on their return from Ngwangwa for another futile consultation with a traditional medicine man. They had stopped at Mtalika to see Dr Mitsitsi, Pangapatha's old friend. The doctor took one look at his friend and gave him a hospital bed. It was while he was admitted that Pangapatha started talking about his brother Sigele Jika, who worked in town. She phoned him at her husband's insistence.

36

Sigele came the following morning to find her and the nurse syringing the patient. By this time Pangapatha was so weak he couldn't even clean his ears.

Atupele caught Sigele several times looking at her closely. She knew why: it was the sores on her wrists and ankles. She didn't mind the inspection. She couldn't help them anyway: her husband had given them to her. At first, it was STDs, followed by tests. Then the sores. Pretty soon they would have to go for VCT and then they'd be on ARVs. That's what Pangapatha was afraid of. He didn't want to learn the truth. Hence all this running around from clinic to clinic to traditional medicine men covering half the country. Even Dr Mitsitsi advised them strongly to go for thorough tests at one of the big hospitals in Kamba.

They went to the big hospital. Pangapatha was admitted immediately. Atupele phoned Sigele, but the man was not responsive. She had to phone him again when Pangapatha died a few days later. He was the only person she had met who could help with the funeral arrangements. Ndamo, her father-in-law, was only a subsistence farmer in Njati district. Her own father was dead. Her mother would not go that far to help. Sigele, strangely enough, complied. He came with his pick-up and took over the funeral arrangements.

It was in these encounters that Atupele found Sigele appealing, yes, that was the word, not attractive. The man was about her father's age, going bald, and rather flabby around the middle. It had something to do with his eyes. Something hesitant, if not restless, like a bird that had not yet decided on which branch to build its nest. Yes, that's it. Nothing furtive, but filled with wonder all the same, something that made Atupele feel as if she wanted to help him build that nest. Yes, aid him.

Then it wouldn't be fair to let him touch her. Atupele couldn't allow Sigele to … She would have to tell him the truth. About Pangapatha's death … About the sores … She could imagine the impact it would have on him, if he came, at all.

Let's break this custom, Atupele would say to him.

It's for your sake, he would respond.

My sake? It doesn't mean anything to me, just a violation of my body, that's all.

Why don't you really want to go through with it?

It's dangerous, I tell you.

Where's the danger?

It's been spreading STDs down the ages and now the deadly AIDS.

It's between consenting adults. They should know their sero-status.

Some of them don't and kill each other as a result. This kusudzula business will wipe out families and villages. The entire nation is at risk.

Do you know your sero-status?

I do. I'm HIV positive. Atupele had gone for VCT while at the hospital. The man there even told her what the sores were: Kaposi's Sarcoma, he said.

Why didn't you tell the elders this?

Do you think they'll understand? All they're interested in is for the custom to go on. I tried arguing with mother, she almost banished me.

Well, I certainly can't go through with it, now. I suspected it all along, seeing the sores all over your limbs.

I knew you knew.

What are we going to do now?

Tell them we did it.

But that'd be a lie.

Look, my husband died of AIDS, you know that. I'll be dying of AIDS pretty soon. too. Do you want to follow suit? What about your wife?

It'd be a small start, Atupele thought. Just the two of them severing the custom. Perhaps the elders would know, by and by, and the reasons why. Perhaps they would come up with a substitute rite. Something to symbolize the act without flesh meeting flesh. Perhaps.

Yes, Atupele was determined now. She would tell Sigele the truth. The elders can bury their outdated custom together with Pangapatha out there under the *nkhadzi* trees. It only starts with one or two. The rest would follow, however long it might take them.

6

Atupele shivered when she heard the rubber soles thump on the bare earth outside. The footsteps approached Agogo's hut. There was no "*Odi*," only the feet sliding through the open door. The shadow deepened the darkness in the room. Atupele wondered fleetingly if the outside fire had been stoked again. She couldn't see it from where she lay. How she could think of it at that time she couldn't fathom. Then the door was shut. It felt as though her heart was also closing against itself.

"*Alamu*," the voice reached across the void.

No answer. Atupele's arms glued her knees together where she shrank on the bed.

"*Alamu*," the form cleared its throat. Atupele jerked up. She had come to recognize Sigele's cough and clearing of the vocal passage before he spoke.

"Who are you?"

"It's Ndakulapa, in-law."

"What are you doing here?" Atupele sprang to her feet almost screaming. She trembled at the knees and slumped down again. "Where is Sigele?"

"Gone. Let me explain."

Atupele tightened her *chitenje* and the grip on it. She felt around the table for the matches. She almost crushed the flimsy box as she pulled out a stick with hands that had suddenly become nerveless. She struck once. Then again. A flare this time. She waved the flame around and saw the indistinct figure in front of her. It was not Sigele. She strangled a scream. She shook her burnt fingers to cool them. She reached out for another stick, struck it and held it against the wick of the tin lamp. The flame almost died out with the force of being pressed down. It wavered but caught. The room was filled with a ghostly glow.

"You're not Sigele." She sobbed hysterically. The elders had cheated her again in the choice of men. All her life it was the elders deciding for her. She had been shunted around from one initiation to another, as if she was a ritual object. No one asked her what her wishes were. What she really felt inside. Now this strange man.

"I'm his older brother." Ndakulapa stepped nearer. "It's like this …."

"Stay where you are!" Atupele swallowed and choked.

Ndakulapa did not obey the instructions. He pulled the folding chair and sat down instead. He turned in the chair and faced her. Atupele's rage threatened to explode inside her. If the elders were playing around with her again like this, someone must be made to pay for it.

"Well," Atupele said limply as she lay back. "Do what you came for."

She closed her eyes. Gritted her teeth and tried to relax but couldn't. She was conscious of every moment but could not respond. She wasn't meant to. It was like this at the *kuchotsa fumbi*, too: the inability to relax and be ready for the performance.

"Your heart wasn't there," Ndakulapa said afterwards.

"It couldn't be," Atupele mumbled groggily. "It's as they say, just a ritual, isn't it? Something anyone could do or should go through to the next stage. Only it was my turn this time. Why me? Why you? As a matter of fact, I haven't even looked at you properly. I don't know you in the way I know Sigele."

"What difference does it make?" Ndakulapa had gone back to the little chair and sat down "He'd have done what I did."

"No, he wouldn't have," Atupele said, emphatically.

"You have doubts about his manhood?" Ndakulapa almost snorted.

"No, not that. He looks quite virile to me" Atupele didn't feel embarrassed to be covered only in a *chitenje* with her underclothes at her feet. In fact, she felt strangely liberated, as if she had just emerged from a cocoon. Maybe the elders were right about the rite, after all. "It's only that I'd have told him the truth. It's the truth that would have stopped him from going on with the *kusudzula* you've just done."

"What truth?"

"I'm HIV positive."

"You're what? Then why ...?

"Exactly. It's my way of telling the elders they shouldn't have done what they did to me. Even my husband. He shouldn't have done what he did to me, at all." Maybe cocoon was not the right image. Perhaps, the *chelule* bird fluttering around in a maze of branches that were confining her, then suddenly finding an opening to escape from man's trap. This image was more appropriate.

"What's all this about? What are you getting at?"

"When I ran away with Pangapatha I imagined a world where men loved their women. Indeed, Pangapatha loved me in his own way. At first. Then came the STDs, the tests, and now this. You haven't looked at me closely, have you? You only came in this morning for the burial. Well, if you had looked at me as closely as Sigele did, you would have noticed the sores on my wrists, and ankles. But you didn't. Even when you came into this room and I lit the lamp. Sigele knew and, as you say, he's gone. Now you know why he's gone."

"You mean Sigele let me take his place knowing you had AIDS?'

"I don't know how Jikas treat each other. What I know is how my husband treated me. If the husband whom I loved killed me in this way, then I shouldn't have a conscience returning the unwanted gift back to the family that gave it to me in the first place."

"My own brother!" Ndakulapa almost choked.

"Think of me." Ndakulapa sat upright on the bed. "My own husband. The father of my children."

"My own in-law, too" Ndakulapa didn't seem to have heard her. "You must enjoy this, if you are the one they send to perform the ceremony."

"It's just a service to the family. Nothing personal."

41

"Not the way you came drooling like a mongrel about to mount a bitch on heat."

"There are no emotions involved. Just a rite."

"No emotions? You didn't think of me and my emotions, did you? What do you think I've been through all these years with my husband a walking corpse? Knowing what he did to other women?"

"You're transferring your husband's sins onto me."

"But, in-law, you performed the rite knowing it was somebody else's wife. Haven't you got a wife? What does she think about your speciality?"

"She, too, is a traditional woman. She believes in these rites." Ndakulapa put his elbows on his thighs, hands between his knees and bent over.

"I want to believe in these rites, too, but not when they're killing me and killing us all in the end. If it was you who had AIDS you'd have passed it onto me the same way, right?"

"I wouldn't."

"Really? How very honest. But just think of me. What do you think I felt when you came to me? Yes, entered me...?

"Same thing ... fulfilling a function."

"Go in peace then, my in-law and report to the elders that you have fulfilled your function. I, too, have done what was required of the widow."

Ndakulapa shuffled to his feet. He bent down to look at his trousers as if he could see the virus there already multiplying. He made a guttural sound and stepped up to Atupele as if he would squeeze her out of this world. Atupele sat unmoving throughout. Ndakulapa made another sound and slunk to the door. He opened it and stumbled down the *khonde* step. He left the door open.

Atupele, after a while, roused herself from the bed. She walked on bare feet to close the door. Ndakulapa had melted into the darkness outside. Atupele wondered how the ritual would end now. The fire outside the bereaved's house had definitely gone out. She shut the door and settled back on Agogo's bed in her earlier position: elbows on thighs and bowed head in cupped hands.

The hyena wears darkness

1

Ndamo, seated on his grass *khonde*, gave Agogo's hut across the *kapinga* lawn another questioning glance. He had been doing so since the sun's rays pierced through the mango tree leaves towering over his house. The furrows between his grey eyebrows deepened at each glance. Although it was understood that Ndakulapa would sleep with the widow for the *kusudzula*, the participants were expected to still wake up at a decent time. Now, with the mango tree shadow retreating from the front yard of the bereaved's house, even the children would know Ndakulapa was Atupele's *fisi*, hyena for the widow's cleansing ceremony. Such public knowledge of a supposedly secret rite would only get Ndamo into trouble again with the government projects people.

"Don't you think you should wake them up now?" Perturbation rasped Ndamo's voice as he asked Pumulani, his wife, bustling around in the outhouse they used as a kitchen.

"You should be the one to do it." Pumulani emerged squinting at him in the searing sunlight. She was a thin angular woman with *nchoma* tattoos on both cheeks. She had a *biriwita* wrapper tied with a cloth belt around the waist.

"I can't do it." He declined the invitation. "Atupele is my daughter-in-law."

"So is she mine," she said pointedly, shaking her head.

They both directed their gaze across the intervening grass expanse to Agogo's hut.

"This is a distressing business," Ndamo declared. "How can they embarrass us like this? Where is Atupele's mother?"

"Having breakfast in the kitchen." Pumulani unrolled the mat she had left on the *khonde* and sat on it. "She said she's leaving as soon as she's finished. You didn't expect her to go over there, did you?"

45

"Who else will do it?" He waved his arms around. When he was trying to contain his thoughts or emotions he pulled his mouth muscles back, at the same time puffing his cheeks. "The kids shouldn't be involved in this."

"Even if it's her daughter in there," Pumulani pointed out, "Andaunire is our visitor here."

"I will do it then." Ndamo ground his teeth pulling back his closed lips. "Even though Ndakulapa is my nephew, he is supposed to report to us."

Ndamo made a show of getting up from the cane chair, then going down the steps of the *khonde* on to the grass. He smarted at being corrected by his wife on a point of protocol. He was also full of misgivings about permitting the cleansing ceremony to go ahead when he was on the project's village committee. The project people, together with the village committee members at several workshops, had identified traditional customs deemed hazardous to health. *Kusudzula,* the widow's sexual cleansing, *kuchotsa fumbi*, the deflowering of initiates, and *kulowa kufa*, wife inheritance were clearly at the top of the risk list. And here he was supervising *kusudzula* right after Pangapatha, his son, was buried yesterday.

The door to Agogo's hut squeaked open. Ndamo, about to climb the single step up to it, checked and stepped aside. Atupele, the widow herself, emerged hesitantly, then slipped just outside the door. She wore the same blue spotted *chitenje* of yesterday with a blouse in a darker shade. As a sign of respect for the young woman, Ndamo sat on the *khonde* to one side of the doorway. Atupele shifted to the other side and knelt down. This positioning made it easier for both to converse without having to face each other directly. There was an awkward silence. Ndamo cleared his throat resolutely.

"You have slept well, my daughter?"

"Very well, father" Atupele sniffed.

A hesitant pause again followed by another question: "Is my nephew still sleeping?" His head inclined in the direction from where she had surfaced.

46

"I slept alone." Atupele bowed her head.

"You what …?" Ndamo jerked upright.

"He left last night …." Atupele averted her eyes. Her voice trailed off tremulously.

"Did he …?" Ndamo stopped himself; he couldn't throw such an intimate question at his own daughter-in-law. It would be another breach of protocol.

Atupele started sobbing quietly. Ndamo ground his teeth, perplexed. He was quite relieved to see Mrs Andaunire coming, closely followed by Pumulani.

"What is it, my daughter?" The two older women joined Atupele on the *khonde*, away from Ndamo.

"Don't start us crying again."

"My nephew didn't sleep in there," Ndamo volunteered when Andaunire's question was only received with heaving, shuddering sobs.

"Then where did he sleep?" Pumulani looked around.

"He couldn't have slept in the bereaved's house," Ndamo said.

"He wasn't supposed to. He doesn't know anybody around to have slept anywhere else."

"It's not a matter of where he slept," Ndamo snapped. "Where is he now? He can't be sleeping wherever he is."

"He couldn't have gone home without bidding us farewell," Pumulani responded.

Ndamo turned to Atupele. "What happened last night?"

Atupele's sobs turned into full-throated wails. Ndamo quailed visibly. He wouldn't make any headway like this. As custom demanded, the older women joined in the lamentations. "Pangapatha! Iih!" "Who am I going to stay with? Pangapatha?" "Oh! My mother!" Ndamo simmered where he sat: soon the whole compound would be filled with more wailing women. Ndamo came to a decision. He stood up and signaled to Pumulani to follow him. He waited for her a short distance away. Pumulani came and knelt down in front of him.

"When Atupele has calmed down find out what really happened last night. I will check on Ndakulapa from the *adzukulu* over there." He turned in the direction of the bereaved's house. He proceeded across the grass. The wailing women behind him reminded him of Pangapatha's funeral yesterday.

He had known Pangapatha was dying when he visited him in hospital at Kamba the week before. It was only a matter of how soon. The doctors couldn't tell him what was killing his son, but Ndamo had guessed. Some of his relatives and nieces looked just as wasted and shrunk as Pangapatha before they finally died. Then three days ago Atupele brought her husband's body in Sigele Jika's pick-up. There were no hitches till the question came up of which male relative would perform the cleansing ceremony with the widow.

Sigele Jika, being Ndamo's nephew and the deceased's brother, was the most likely candidate. Although very reluctant he would have complied till Ndakulapa, the older brother showed up. Sigele, then conveniently abdicated his role to Ndakulapa, pointing out that the elder was the Jika family's *nkhoswe* in traditional transactions. The elders had assented to the switch of hyenas. Ndakulapa had then taken over the proceedings. But now it seemed as if Ndakulapa, too, had abdicated. Being a three-day ceremony the rite was incomplete. Why had Ndakulapa accepted the role of hyena in the first place, then?

The bereaved's house was long emptied of ordinary mourners and sympathizers. Busy inside, though, were the *adzukulu* from the neighboring villages, who were responsible for preparing the body and the graveyard. What was remaining this morning was to mop the walls and floors of the bereaved's house with medicated water to clear it of spirits and witches. Ndamo found the oldest one supervising in the next room.

"Did you see Ndakulapa here last night?"

"As you can see, we are only the *adzukulu* here. The rest have gone till the *lumeto*, shaving of hair tomorrow."

"He couldn't have gone to Fikani." Ndamo retraced his steps but headed for his own house this time. Things seemed to have quietened down at Agogo's hut. Pumulani found Ndamo in his former place soon afterward. As before, she sat on the mat.

"He didn't sleep there either" Ndamo reported.

"This is the work of witchcraft," Pumulani opined "It's unheard of to abandon the rite on the first night. Perhaps he didn't know that ...."

"It's not his first time, even in Mutopa," Ndamo cut her short.

Mutopa village was not so-named for nothing. It was the village mourning. In the past, the deaths were attributed to witchcraft. In recent years, it was because of what the villagers called "the government disease," AIDS, on account of the intervention from that quarter. The deaths had become regular, too. That was one of the reasons the government project people had selected Mutopa for its pilot workshops on HIV&AIDS. The focus was on hazardous traditional practices. The elders' counterarguments were: with what were they to replace them since they were so well-established? The project people had advised: let's work together to find ways of turning these customs into positive weapons of change.

"We'll have a scandal on our hands." Pumulani wrung her hands. "We'll be the laughing stock of Mutopa. What will the people say when they hear that our hyena fled the ritual hut in the night?"

"We'll have a scandal of a different kind," Ndamo corrected. "What will the project people say when they hear that our committee members consented to the ritual behind their backs? All the plans for the orphan care and skills center will be canceled now."

"Don't believe everything those people promise you. Mutopa will be as it was before they came."

"You don't know anything," Ndamo scoffed. "Look at Gawani village. They not only built a skills center there, they transformed the path into a road connecting it to the main one. They brought in water pumps. There's now talk of building a clinic there."

"Let them build those things there!" Pumulani brushed him aside. "Who are the project people to tell us what to do in our own land?

Without the cleansing ceremonies, we will have more deaths in Mutopa. Just imagine different groups of mourners passing each other twice on the same day, one from a burial, the other to the next."

"Those are the kinds of beliefs the project people want to discourage. These cleansing ceremonies are the real cause of disease, they maintain."

"They are the kind of beliefs that sustained our forefathers," Pumulani put in impatiently: "We have been through this before, my husband. We didn't establish the customs ourselves, today or yesterday. We found them. We inherited them. They, too, inherited them from their forefathers, passed on from generation to generation. How can the project people believe we can abandon our customs just because they'll build us a road to the *boma*?"

"What are we going to do now?" Ndamo cut her ramblings short.

"We have a crisis on our hands. The only thing that'll save us is to find your nephew and bring him back here!" Pumulani then grew more conspiratorial. "He's got to complete the ceremony. The young man did it only once and fled without explanation."

Ndamo's lips and cheeks grew very agitated. "But having fled from here, what will make him return and be laughed at?"

"You know the alternative is to hire a *namandwa* – the professional hyena – and start all over again."

"Those people cost a lot of money; we can't afford it."

"Exactly and we want to keep the ceremony within the family. So it has to be your nephew. Which means today. The shaving of the hair is tomorrow. And Andaunire is breathing fire again. She is threatening to take us to court for breaking our part of the ceremony."

Andaunire had brought the appropriate medicines all the way from Mbamba, her lakeshore home. In fact, she was the one who had pressurized them *kusudzula* Atupele the night of her husband's burial.

"Do you know what this means?" Ndamo almost yelped. "I will have to catch a bus to Fikani and back."

"What else can we do? You're his uncle, the only one he will listen to."

"All for the sake of cleansing a widow?"

"You and I know that *kusudzula* is more than cleansing the widow. The union of man and woman brought us all into the world. We are severing the bond that tied the husband and wife together. You can't have a spirit tied to a living person. It will cause havoc for her and the whole community."

"This is a very depressing business." Ndamo pulled back his lips. "Here we are, wallowing between what the ancestors taught us to revere and what the tribe has to do to survive. Half of me says: do what is right by your forefathers. The other says: do what is right for your people, the ancestors will understand."

"You don't have only your forefathers to contend with. Right now, Andaunire is coming to find out what you are going to do about her daughter."

"Tell her I'm on my way." Ndamo pulled himself together. He found Andaunire a formidable woman. He did not want another confrontation with her. He had consented to every suggestion she had made. It had resulted in shortening the period of the cleansing ceremony. She also had shortened the period she could stay after burial. She had declared she wasn't even going to stay for the *lumeto*. That was for Atupele, she said. I've a business to look after at Mbamba. Potential violence bubbled under her imposing frame. Each time she turned a baleful eye to him, he quivered inwardly. He caught the same expression on her face as she advanced purposefully towards his house.

"I have got to change." Ndamo got up precipitately "I can't be taking buses and making visits in these tatters."

2

Ndakulapa didn't know whether to bellow like a wounded buffalo or whimper like a mongrel that had received a whack on its behind. He erupted from Agogo's hut, stumbled, and almost fell down the step that led him onto the level ground outside. The tropical night draped his form like a black shroud as he got his bearings on the *kapinga* grass that separated Agogo's hut, the bereaved's house, and Uncle Ndamo's. He couldn't go into the bereaved's house to join other mourners on their second day of the wake. He certainly wasn't going back to Uncle Ndamo's house. He wasn't expected to report on how the *kusudzula* ceremony had gone with Atupele, the widow. He just couldn't face anyone after what had happened in Agogo's hut that night or even the morning after. In the end, he slunk away from Mutopa like a marauding hyena that had been thwarted of its prey.

It wasn't that Uncle Ndamo and the elders weren't expecting an immediate report. It was that Atupele had given a medical report he wasn't prepared to present to anyone, now or perhaps ever. There was a devastating message involved.

"I am HIV positive," she had announced soon after their sex cleansing session. She said she was only returning the compliments to the family that had produced Pangapatha, who had infected her in the first place. Ritual or no ritual, how does an infected *fisi* report a message like that?

He had trembled where he stood, his bones shook inside him, and his manhood shrank between his legs. He wanted to scream, whimper, groan, roar, but only the enormity of the news grew in the darkness confronting him. He even started hearing the funeral songs that had been sung that afternoon escorting Pangapatha, the widow's husband and his own cousin. They were now being sung for him.

Confused by this turn of events, Ndakulapa caught the late bus home. In transit, he swung between volcanic shudders and simpering sighs that made the other passengers shrink away from him fearfully. This turbulent state fueled him for the whole trip to Fikani village. It was almost midnight when Nansani, his wife, opened the door. She was clad in a *chitenje* only.

"What is it, father of Mwaona?" Nansani asked. She had lit a paraffin lamp before opening the door. She wasn't too sleepy to notice the murderous mood he was in. Ndakulapa brushed past her and slumped onto a chair. He cupped one fist in the palm of the other hand and pushed. The knuckles cracked rapidly one after another: krr! krrr!

krr! He switched round and cracked the knuckles of the other hand. Krr! krr! krr! ricocheted in the room. He breathed noisily.

"How did the funeral go?" Nansani asked hesitantly from another chair round the small table meant for four people.

"Don't ask stupid questions. How do funerals go: fine or badly?"

Ndakulapa's roar seemed to fling Nansani backward in her chair. When she recovered slightly she ventured again. "Shall I cook something for you? I wasn't expecting you tonight so I didn't keep …."

"When were you expecting me? Just go back to bed, woman." Nansani fled. A doorless wooden frame separated her from her husband's wrath. She sat on the mat beside the single bed that was the only furniture. She cowered in the dark, wondering what was coming next.

In the front room, Ndakulapa leaned his elbows on top of the small table. The fists which now supported his forehead closed his eyes, they hurt. He remained in that position, reviewing the events of the past twelve hours.

Ndakulapa got the news of Pangapatha's death just yesterday morning. He boarded a bus for Njati soon afterward, to be in time for the burial. Sigele Jika, his younger brother, was already at Mutopa, having transported the corpse and the widow there. In fact, Ndakulapa could trace his present predicament to Sigele and his refusal to be the relative-on-the-spot for the widow's *kusudzula*. At the last moment, Sigele had abdicated his appointment, pointing out that it was Ndakulapa's duty to fulfill the hyena's role, now that he was present, since he was the Jika family's *nkhoswe*. The elders assented. Ndakulapa met his nemesis that way.

Ndakulapa's mind seethed with all the options before him. Now that he was infected, should he tell his wife the truth? If he didn't tell her, would he infect her, too? If he kept quiet but did not fulfill his conjugal obligations, what explanation would he give her? How long could he keep away from her before she started questioning or even importuning? He had told Atupele that Nansani was also steeped in traditional customs, but did his wife actually know that he was a hyena?

53

Unlike others, one didn't advertise the hyena profession. Although the elders appointed him because of his manifest prowess to begin with, they too did not declare publicly who was on their staff list. Hyenas, wearing the mantle of darkness, worked quietly, routinely cleansing their community of their iniquities. The coming of AIDS now threw the hyena practice into terrible disarray. Before it, they could go to the clinical officer or the medicine man for the smaller diseases. They got cured and continued their trade, their wives were none the wiser. But AIDS spelt sure death.

Ndakulapa had seen Nkalawire, his niece, break into spots and then develop a terrible cough. Thereafter, they had watched her waste and shrink under their very eyes. In the end, the once robust woman weighed no more than a little girl. Nkalawire was not the only case. Fikani had come to routinely bury their dead; they knew who suffered from the government disease, but even though alive, the patients tried to hide their status.

But then if one refused to perform the rites there were always the *namandwa,* those professional ritual cleansers the people could turn to. So what was one to do now? Perhaps if he consulted Atsalaachaje, their local medicine man, right away, he could do it. Atsalaachaje was no mean choice. He plied his trade with the village and town. After his initial successes in Fikani and the neighboring villages, he had opened some clinics in Kamba city's townships. He specialized not only in bodily ailments but also vanities: success in love, business, and the workplace. His regular customers were executives, managers, directors, shop-owners, contractors, and the like. Ndakulapa was a regular customer, to keep his tools of the trade always in working order.

Ndakulapa removed the knuckles from his closed eyes. The release of pressure hurt him as well. He sighed deeply and roused himself from the chair. Yes, he must go to Atsalaachaje before it was too late. He joined his wife in the next room as the second cock crowed.

The following morning found Ndakulapa saying the customary "Odi" in Atsalaachaje's front yard. Unlike others, the grass fence that enclosed his compound started in the middle of both sides of the main house. The fence itself had side doors that served as both entrances and exits. Atsalaachaje used the sitting room as the consultation room.

This arrangement proved awkward when other patients were present. If you needed more private ministrations you made a special request. The man then took you outside to one corner of the house. Ndakulapa knew the routine and did not waste time with the preambles.

"Hyenas like you need protective medicine not only *nkhondokubedi* potency potions." Atsalaachaje was quite forthright with his patient. He wore ordinary clothes: a short-sleeved shirt; a pair of khaki trousers and sandals. He was as old as Ndamo but with darker and drier skin stretched over aged limbs.

"Do you have anything for this government disease?"

"If I was another kind of medicine man I would have given you an easy antidote going around these days."

"What's that?"

"It's like a cleansing ritual to get rid of the infection."

"What's done?"

"You sleep with your own daughter or niece. They have to be yours, of course, preferably virgins, too."

"I couldn't possibly do that."

"Come on, it's like *kuchotsa fumbi* and you have done it before. It's part of your work. In the night, you don't know who you're deflowering: a daughter, a niece, or someone unrelated to you. They all open their legs without declaring their names. You leave as anonymously as you came. No one knows it's you, their father or uncle during the day."

"But in this case, I'd be known."

"I am not prescribing you that. I doubt if it works at all. It's just a license for incest if you ask me."

"Then do you have anything that works?" Ndakulapa implored, "because if you don't, this spells the death of hyenas. No hyena will continue working anymore in the face of AIDS."

"Frankly, my friend, we have no cure for it. Don't let anyone fool you on this. At first, we thought AIDS was *magawagawa*. So we treated it as such. Too late, we realized it wasn't, and we had no traditional answers for it. So we changed tactics. The same government that gave us AIDS brought ARVs. So what we do is to mix the *magawagawa* potions with the ARVs. It gives our patients more confidence that way. At least, they live longer than they would if they didn't take the concoction."

"Do you have them?"

"You don't have to get them from me. You would only have to pay me, when they are free in any government clinic."

"But that means being tested first, doesn't it?"

"Of course, they don't just hand them out like aspirin, you know"

"But for your patients it's a mixed formula, not so?"

"They are the ones who insist on it. They believe the old mixed with the new will cure them definitely. I comply; give the customer what he believes in. That's halfway towards curing him."

"Give me the mixed stuff, then. I've got to have it now while the virus doesn't know what to do with me. If I wait for testing at the clinic, it will have settled in its new home."

"You see?" Atsalaachaje laughed. "You are the one insisting on the modified formula."

Atsalaachaje left Ndakulapa to go inside. He returned with a jugful of some liquid and a packet. "Take this now," he said with a smile, "Since you are so desperate. The rest you take as prescribed at the clinic."

Ndakulapa took the first gulp and nearly choked. Atsalaachaje laughed. He watched his patient grimace and with grim determination drink the rest down.

"Have you heard of the *nansanganya*?" Atsalaachaje asked, retrieving his jug.

Ndakulapa's face was still twitching with distaste. "Is that it?"

"No. *Nansanganya* is the stuff the chiefs are using now for *kusudzula* and a few other rites."

"How can they do that? *Nansanganya* is only used for young initiates to protect them for the outdooring."

"Exactly. It has now been adapted to protect you fellows and widows from infectious diseases."

"What is the world coming to? Do these chiefs have proper *anankungwi*? The man's and woman's fluids must mingle and go to the bones. When the man withdraws, he draws out all her iniquities, too. That's what our forefathers told us."

"The chiefs are accepting the new modified version to protect their people. A chief is a chief because he protects his people, that is, living people. The people are dying with our *kusudzula, kuchotsa fumbi,* and *kulowa kufa* because that's where they are getting the AIDS from, like you have done. What does it profit a chief if he rules an empty village? Given the choice of death or adaptation, the chiefs have opted for life."

"They must be progressive chiefs, then."

"They are. These things are happening now all around you. I'm now making quite a lot of business with *nansanganya*. I'm telling you this as one of my regular customers. Now that this thing has happened to you, I would think seriously about it. Talk to your relatives about it. You don't want them wiped out, too, because of you and your profession."

Ndakulapa left Atsalaachaje in as confused a state as he had come earlier. He reached home not knowing what to do next. He took the grass entrance to the back of his house. He shivered violently as if he had malaria when he saw Uncle Ndamo waiting for him on the *khonde*.

3

Ndamo arrived at Fikani village just before noon. He wore a gray shirt and faded black trousers. Light brown socks and brown shoes covered his feet. He had taken time to comb his sparse gray hair, too. The slight frown still sat between his brows. He was perched on a chair on the *khonde*.

After the preliminaries of greeting a surprised Nansani, he was given boiled sweet potatoes to be washed down with black tea. They didn't talk much after. Nansani busied herself in the outhouse. Once she went out of the grass fence with a bucket. She apologized profusely for leaving the visitor alone. She came back with water. There were no children around. Ndamo was left to his own devices while waiting for his nephew. From his elevated position, he had a view of the outhouses and bath-shed enclosed by the grass fence surrounding the back of the house. Through the entrance of the fence he could see a *nandolo* and maize garden. It was from the path alongside this garden that he saw Ndakulapa approaching.

Ndakulapa always reminded his uncle of grinding stones with the *mwanamphero* mate perched on top of it. Ndakulapa was of medium height with a small round head on top of disproportionately broad shoulders linked by a short neck. Ndamo quickly reviewed Ndakulapa's bewildering behavior the past few hours. It was so unprecedented the forefathers had not laid down what course of action to take should it occur. Ndamo stood up and went down the step. It was a considerably agitated nephew he now met.

"Uncle Ndamo," Ndakulapa said in a shaky voice. They shook hands, then Ndakulapa hastily disengaged himself. He turned and lifted the chair from the *khonde* to set it on level ground beside where Ndamo stood uncertainly.

"Sit down here. I will sit there." Ndakulapa sat himself on the bare *khonde* floor. Ndamo, after hesitating briefly, sat down again. Ndakulapa seemed to be struggling with a multitude of horrors threatening to tear his insides apart. Ndamo, on the other hand, looking like a living question, barely suppressed himself.

"You have traveled well, uncle?" Ndakulapa finally controlled himself to a communicable level.

"As safely as the bus driver allowed us to arrive in one piece." Ndamo looked at the other critically. "I see you arrived well, too".

Ndakulapa shifted uneasily where he sat, his face muscles working. He put his elbows on his thighs and passed his palm flat against his face as if to wipe out some terrifying vision. Then he pushed both palms to the sides of his face and hooked the thumbs behind the ears. He inhaled audibly.

"I must have left tracks of shame for you to find me so soon ... so early, I was going to say."

"Only an incomplete job," Ndamo said simply. "There was only one place you could come back to."

"You find me in my hour of shame, having abandoned the widow."

"There is a lot we have got to discuss, my son," he puffed his cheeks by pulling his closed lips back.

"You sent me to my death." Ndakulapa whispered, shuddering.

"What are you talking about?" Ndamo leaned forward.

"The woman you gave me is death." Ndakulapa straightened his arms and held them clasped between his thighs. "I left last night without bidding farewell to anyone to avoid another death."

"What death?" Ndamo's forehead knitted.

"Actually killing!" He clenched his fists. "I'd have strangled that woman."

"Atupele? Why?"

"She succeeded in killing me." An almost deranged laugh came out as Ndakulapa held his forehead helplessly.

"Can you please explain clearly what you're trying to tell me?" Ndamo stood and clasped his nephew's shoulder.

"The grave where I am going to be buried has already been measured and laid out for me. It is only waiting for the diggers to start their job. Each day they'll call out for me to come and enter the hole so they can go and rest. Each day they'll wait for the walking corpse to come to his grave. My days are numbered. Atupele infected me with HIV. Soon I'll have AIDS and follow Pangapatha." Ndakualapa sat down heavily.

Ndamo sat down too, suddenly. "It can't be. How do you know?"

"She told me herself, afterward of course."

"You mean Pangapatha died of AIDS?

"Don't pretend you didn't know," Ndakulapa snarled. "You and the elders knew it but you sent me to her. I wasn't even supposed to be the hyena on this death. Sigele knew it and bolted. You all conspired to kill me through that woman."

"You are the *nkhoswe* of the family and there was no way we could have known …"

"Don't lie to me, otherwise I will really kill someone to accompany me to the grave."

Ndamo was too stunned to talk. Ndakulapa went on furiously.

"You visited your son in hospital. The doctors must have told you what was wrong with him."

Rather than risk another shut up Ndamo only shook his head. Ndakulapa went on relentlessly.

"The *adzukulu* prepared the body under your supervision. You lied to the church elders. You lied to the people. You lied …"

Ndakulapa shook where he sat. Ndamo cowered in his chair.

"This is a sorry business." His cheeks went up and down. "I was sent to bring you back."

"The only reason I will go back is to kill that witch," he hissed savagely.

"Stop blaming Atupele. My daughter-in-law is really a much-abused woman. Just imagine her husband dying on her. And there we were inflicting a strange man on her, on top of her tragic loss. How do you think all this affected her?"

"Should I feel remorse after what she did to me deliberately?"

"Like you and me, Atupele was only a victim of a rite that's threatening to wipe us all out. The least we can do is to make amends and try to reconcile with her. And you are the key person in this matter."

"I am the key person to my own death." Ndakulapa raved. "I went to her with my eyes wide open. Ach! This ritual is killing us all: First

Pangapatha, then me. Next will be my wife, too. I don't know who else after that."

"That's it!" Ndamo changed tactics. "This might be the ancestors telling us to stop the rite now."

"How could the ancestors establish the custom and then come round to tell us to stop it?"

"We need to understand what is happening to us," Ndamo said earnestly. "This is what the project people have been telling us all along. Our ancestors didn't have AIDS to contend with. Now there is AIDS and it is killing their children. They are telling us it's time to stop all this. Or as the project people are saying, if that's difficult, to at least modify some of the customs before they destroy us."

"What do you mean?" Ndakulapa remembered Atsalaachaje's remarks earlier.

"At the last meeting of the council of elders we agreed to modify *kusudzula* by having the hyena and the widow go through a symbolic act of cleansing. There would be no direct contact."

"Then why did you let me go through the real method?" Ndakulapa asked wrathfully.

"Pangapathu died soon after the meeting," Ndamo told him hastily. "He had to be buried. Mrs Andaunire came with her medicines and pressured me to go on with the old hyena business. Everything happened so fast I was going to announce the modified method tomorrow at the *lumeto* ceremony."

"It's too late for me now. I am already infected. I am caught between the old and new methods. Either way I am dying."

"Not really." Ndamo shook his head vehemently. "The project people have what they call ARVs. These are medicines for infected people, they say. If they can't cure AIDS they at least give you long life. With them and at your age, you'll live your natural life span."

"This is what Atsalaachaje was trying to tell me."

"Who is Atsalaachaje?"

Ndakulapa explained between shudders and deep exhalations. When he had finished Ndamo got him by the shoulders again.

"You see?" he pointed out excitedly. "It's happening everywhere, even here. We were slow to catch on in Mutopa."

"What you are trying to tell me," Ndakulapa said wearily "is that you and the elders have already been convinced to abolish the custom that sustained our ancestors?"

"Not to abolish but to modify them."

"Abolish or modify, what difference does it make? They are still being changed. This is a betrayal of the people by our trusted chiefs, headmen and elders. You sold us to the project people. We are defeated without even striking a blow. You, our elders, are now at the forefront persuading us and supervising how to change our customs."

"Exactly, we need everyone to help us to protect our people. In this case change is life. It is for the survival of the people. So will you please help, too?"

"In what way can I help you now?" Ndakulapa rasped indignantly. "You are propagating a symbolic method that needs no direct contact. To me this spells my symbolic death. It is death to all hyenas."

"On the contrary, the hyenas continue their important role of cleansing the widow. They are crucial to the symbolic act. With this method, in the face of AIDS, we are saving both the widows and the hyenas. They survive to resume their ordinary roles as mothers and fathers in their own families."

"You know very well I did not apply for this job," Ndakulapa simmered: "You, the elders and my people, asked me to perform certain duties. You challenged us: where are our young men who can do this for us? Has their manhood been smashed falling from pawpaw trees? Has the hare run between their legs, rendering them impotent? Do we have to hire a *namandwa* to do the job for them? I answered the challenge and now look at me."

"Precisely. You are here because of the society's need for your services. Although you don't sit on the council of elders you are a very, very important person to us. You are as important as the *adzukulu*, those people the same elders run to in times of bereavement to prepare the corpses and graveyards for us since we can't do it ourselves. In fact, as you very well know, your cleansing job starts right after the *adzukulu* have finished theirs. What the people are asking you now, through me, is to continue your work as before."

"Even with this so called modified symbolic version?"

"Even because of it. The only difference is that you will now be working during the day and not concealed by darkness as before."

"It'll be a new kind of hyena then," Ndakulapa pointed out ruefully. He reflected on the new role he had to play now. Being a successful hyena meant also being on good terms with the elders. They were the ones who assigned the duties. If they were modifying the customs, then their hyenas had to do the same. That was the only way to survive in the changed, difficult circumstances. Even Atsalaachaje was modifying his concoctions.

"Yes," Ndamo assented, gravely, "one that can now sit side by side with the elders, openly involved in the affairs of the people. In fact, with your experience you can help us convert the people and the other hyenas by pointing out what you have been through. When you open your mouth, you will be speaking from the depths of your heart. It will make the message more meaningful, credible, and urgent."

"As you say or as your project people say," Ndakulapa was pensive, "our ancestors didn't have AIDS confronting them. If they had had AIDS, it would have forced them to rethink their own traditions, too." He remembered Atupele's words last night: she said she, too, wanted to believe in the rite, but not when it was killing us all. They were now appealing to him to do something to rectify the situation. Ndakulapa was angry, but couldn't hang it on anyone in particular.

"We have been seriously rethinking some of our customs after each workshop. We've come to realize more and more that we are all contributing to the mess we are in. In truth, veiled personal interests hide behind the stuff we claim to be customs. What is *kuchotsa fumbi* but man's license to be the first one to take the virgins before anyone else? What is *kusudzula* but coveting your brother's spouse, really? Some of this covetousness manifests itself in *kulowa kufa*, wife

63

inheritance, which is a public declaration of polygamy. Just think of it, who stands to win in all this? Once you scrutinize these customs, all you see is man's lust, greed, and covetousness."

"But the women also consent to them." Ndakulapa reexamined his own work. He went over the amount of preparation he did on each assignment: including the potency potions, the anticipation of the performance with whoever happened to be the partner. Was that what custom demanded, what the society wanted of him? Or was he fulfilling his own personal desires? Was it his own vested interests that had brought about his own infection?

"Out of fear." Ndamo cleared the mist. "Confronted with the relatives' coercion the widows submit."

"You sound more and more like Atsalaachaje."

"I would like to meet this medicine man of yours."

"I can take you to him before we return to Mutopa. In my new symbolic role of a daylight hyena I will still need his *nansanganya*."

"He'll help us tremendously." Ndamo sighed, his mouth and cheeks working up and down.

THE END

GLOSSARY

Most vernacular words are translated within the text immediately after they occur. However, for the benefit of those who would like to have them at a glance, they appear below. Also, for convenience, the words have been classified by subject matter. Within each category, the words appear in alphabetical order.

A.   Persons

1. *Adzukulu*: Persons responsible for the preparation of a corpse for burial. Not to be confused with the same word for nephews and nieces.

2. *Alamu*: An in-law of either sex, singular: *mlamu*.

3. *Fisi*: Hyena. A person responsible for the ritual sexual cleansing in the community. As such, he is also responsible for the ritual deflowering of female initiates. Not to be confused with the same word for the animal.

4. *Mvano*: a group of women in the CCAP church.

5. *Namandwa*: As in *fisi*, the hyena, above. Only this time he is a professional and comes from outside the family, relatives, or clan.

6. *Nankungwi*: An instructor of either sex responsible for imparting traditional knowledge especially at initiation ceremonies.

7. *Nkhoswe*: A go-between. A person who represents members of a family in any negotiations or transactions.

B.   Customs

1. *Kuchotsa fumbi*: Literally, to remove the dust, usually of the initiation camp from the candidates. Metaphorically, first ritual sex of the candidates as part of the outdooring.

2. *Chisamba*: The initiation at the first pregnancy.

3. *Kulowa kufa*: Widow inheritance at the death of her husband, usually by a brother or a close relative.

4. *Lumeto*: The shaving of the hair after the funeral of a close relative. Also *kumeta* or *m'meto*. Not to be confused with the same word for membership of a *gule wamkulu* or *nyau* cult.

5. *Mwambo*: Traditional beliefs and customs. Plural, *miyambo*. Not to be confused with *miyambi*, proverbs.

6. *Mwikho*: Violation of *mwambo* above. Hence, taboo.

7. *Sadaka*: A feast commemorating the dead.

8. *Kusudzula*: The ritual sexual cleansing of the widow or widower, usually with a close relative. See *fisi* and *namandwa* above.

C.   Flora and fauna

1. *Chelule*: a small bird

2. *Chitimbe*: Pitiostigma thonningii.

3. *Kachere*: Ficus

4. *Kapinga*: Cynodon dactylon

5. *Masuku*: Uapaca kirkiana

6. *Nandolo*: Cajanus cajan

7. *Nkhadzi*: Euphorbia trucalli

(The Latin names are from Blodwen Binns and J P Logah, *Dictionary of Plant Names in Malawi*, 1972)

D.   Ailments and cures

1. *Magawagawa*: An illness characterized by splitting of the skin, especially on the feet. Not to be confused with the same word for a children's game.

2. *Nansanganya*: Literally, mixed drugs, e.g. a cocktail to cure certain illnesses. Not to be confused with the same word for incestuous relationships in a village.

3. *Nkhondokubedi*: Literally, war-in-bed. A potency drug.

E.   Personal enhancement and apparel

1. *Biriwita*: A black wrapper

2. *Chitenje*: A wrapper, usually colourful

3. *Nchoma*: A tattoo, usually on the face

F.   Domestic appliances

1. *Mkeka*: A palm leaf mat

2. *Mwanamphero*: The small stone in a pair of grinding stones

G.   Miscellaneous

1. *Boma*: The district headquarters

2. *Khonde*: The verandah

3. *Odi*: An oral knock, uttered when entering or passing a homestead

Printed in the United States
By Bookmasters